Coo
CHR

JOSCELINE DIMBLEBY

A SAINSBURY COOKBOOK

Published by Woodhead-Faulkner Limited
8 Market Passage, Cambridge CB2 3PF
for J Sainsbury Limited
Stamford House, Stamford Street, London SE1 9LL

First published 1978
Second impression 1979
Third impression 1980
Fourth impression 1981

ISBN 0 85941 101 X

Cover design and text layout: Ken Vail
Colour photography and cover picture: Bryce Attwell

The publishers wish to thank Josiah Wedgwood and Son Limited and Elizabeth David for the loan of some of the china and cookware which appear in the photographs.

Typesetting: Best Typesetting
Printed and bound in Great Britain by
William Clowes (Beccles) Limited, Beccles and London

The Author

Josceline Dimbleby was born in Oxford in 1943. From the age of five her childhood was spent abroad, mostly in the Middle East and South America, so that at an early age she learned to appreciate a wide variety of food.

Josceline's instinct has always been to create her own recipes, which results in varied and interesting dishes, but leading a very busy life herself she appreciates the value of advance preparation and simple methods and most of her recipes reflect this view without in any way affecting their originality.

Josceline regularly writes cookery articles for the national press and has also appeared on television. Her first cookery book, *A Taste of Dreams*, was published by Hodder & Stoughton in 1976 and in 1977 she produced *Party Pieces*, a booklet for the Victoria and Albert Museum's Silver Jubilee Exhibition of Young British Craftsmen. *Cooking for Christmas* is the first of a series of cookery books she is writing for Sainsbury's.

Josceline lives in London with her husband, television personality David Dimbleby, and their three lively children, all of whom, she says, eagerly try out and give constructive criticism on each new dish.

Contents

Introduction

On Christmas Day in medieval England you might have sat down to feast on boar's head, swan pie or roast peacock. These delicacies gave way in their turn to goose, hams and ribs of beef and although the turkey was imported from America in the late sixteenth century it did not take over as a Christmas tradition until Victorian times.

Nowadays we look forward to the ritual of the outsize golden turkey and a flaming Christmas pudding. In a way it is a relief not to have to think too hard what food to have or how to cook it. But then there is a danger of not thinking at all, of just cooking those once-a-year dishes in an automatic way so that they taste just the same, year after year. There are variations which can enliven the taste while keeping within the old traditions. Children love plain turkey but, mainly for the adults, I stuff it with rich and tasty stuffings which I change slightly each year. And although we stick to traditional Christmas pudding and mince pies we have a dark chocolate cake instead of a fruit cake and ice it with soft white frosting, complete with decorations, of course!

However, it is probably not just one blow-out meal you have to produce but more often meals for several days, meals which each in a different way should revive the jaded palate. I hope this book will help you through all those days of eating. I have collected what I feel to be particularly appetising versions of Christmas Day food together with my own ideas for the other days, dishes which can mostly be made well in advance to help you plan and work ahead. This may be an effort but I find that making a list and organising the food in advance down to the last Brussels sprout is the only way I can survive and really enjoy Christmas.

Each Christmas is a performance which everyone in the family will compare with every other Christmas and if you are the cook you are the person most responsible for its success. Yet, quite apart from producing all that food, you must enjoy the festivities yourself, calmly accept the amazing mess the house will get into, find lost presents, make lists for thank-you letters, control the children's over-excitement, break up their fights and smooth over any frictions caused by a long period of family and relations being closeted together.

Nevertheless, these drawbacks cannot prevent Christmas still being for me one of the most exciting times of the year. I even look forward to the cooking, which can be one of the most powerful moments for the family cook. Despite the rival attractions of presents, games, surprises, drink and talk you are the one who can produce the trump card – wonderful food which everyone will remember all year through!

Note: As most people have their family with them at Christmas, most of the quantities in these recipes are for 6–8 people but, of course, you can halve them if there are only a few of you. Quantities of ingredients are given in both metric (g, ml) and imperial (oz, pt) measures: you can use either, *but not a mixture of both*, in any given recipe.

The Christmas Dinner

I feel it's a mistake to think that the special atmosphere of Christmas Day will make this "meal of the year" taste good even if you make very little effort with the real flavour of the food. You must try and make it the best turkey they've ever tasted, with the most succulent stuffings, crisp fresh vegetables, golden crunchy potatoes and not a packet sauce in sight. (Well, if you must use packet bread sauce add more cloves, nutmeg and finely grated onion to it to give it zest!) Your Christmas pudding will be far more moist and crumbly if you make it yourself and you can buy packs of little silver charms to put in the mixture. It's all rather a lot of work, but how can a good Christmas not be – at least a lot of the cooking can be done well in advance and gives me, at any rate, a childish feeling of excited anticipation. More than any other meal, the Christmas dinner has to be planned step by step if you are going to remain calm: however disorganised a person you may be, you surely must write out a true plan of campaign for Christmas morning. This way you will have a much better chance of a relaxed and happy Christmas, leaving everyone with tantalising memories of your spectacular food.

Roast Turkey

Prepare your turkey for roasting the day before. Stuff each end of the bird* and rub lavishly all over with at least $\frac{1}{4}$ lb butter or margarine. Wrap up in well buttered foil and put in a roasting tin. On Christmas Day preheat the oven to Gas Mark 3/325°F/160°C (unless you are doing your roast potatoes in advance – see p. 13). Put the turkey low down in the oven and cook for $2\frac{1}{2}$–3 hours for a 6–8 lb (2.5–3.5 kg) bird, 3–$3\frac{3}{4}$ hours for an 8–14 lb (3.5–6.0 kg) bird and $3\frac{3}{4}$–$4\frac{1}{4}$ hours for a 14–18 lb (6.0–8.0 kg) bird. Three-quarters of an hour before it is ready, unwrap the foil to expose the turkey so that it will brown, and pour a glass of dry vermouth or white wine over it.

After you have transferred the turkey to a carving board make the gravy. Blend 1 rounded teaspoon (2 × 5 ml spoon) of arrowroot or cornflour with a little water and stir into the pan juices. Let this bubble over the heat until thickened and season to taste. Serve the gravy with the turkey, accompanied by cranberry sauce and bread sauce.

*Although many people do stuff both ends of the turkey, overfilling can result in the bird not being thoroughly cooked. Great care should be taken not to put too much stuffing in the body cavity, or the stuffing can be cooked separately and an onion or lemon placed in the bird during cooking.

Roast Turkey with Chestnut Stuffing, Veal, Lemon and Parsley Stuffing, and Spiced Cranberry and Orange Sauce

Stuffings

Although the appearance of the golden turkey is exciting, the taste is often dull. However, if you take the trouble to make two excellent, contrasting stuffings the flavour will be infinitely superior. The Veal, Lemon and Parsley Stuffing should be used to stuff the neck cavity, while the Chestnut Stuffing may be cooked in a baking dish and served separately, or cooked in the body cavity.

Chestnut Stuffing
4 oz (100 g) smoked streaky bacon
2 oz (50 g) butter
1 onion – peeled and chopped finely
turkey heart and liver – chopped finely
6 oz (150 g) sliced mushrooms
10 oz (250 g) chestnut purée
1 small tin or tube of liver pâté
3 large cloves garlic – chopped finely
1 tablespoon (15 ml spoon) dried oregano
2 oz (50 g) fresh breadcrumbs
1 lightly whisked egg
salt, black pepper

Cut the rind off the bacon and chop into small cubes. Put the butter in a pan and fry the bacon, the onion and the turkey heart and liver for 3–5 minutes. Transfer to a bowl with all the fat, stir in all the other ingredients thoroughly with a wooden spoon and season well. Fill baking dish, baste with a little of the turkey juices and place in the oven to cook with the bird for the final ¾ hour.

Veal, Lemon and Parsley Stuffing
6 oz (150 g) minced veal
4 oz (100 g) fresh brown breadcrumbs
grated rind and juice of 1 large lemon
large handful of parsley – chopped finely
4 oz (100 g) melted butter
1 lightly whisked egg
salt, black pepper

Simply mix all the ingredients thoroughly together in a bowl, season well and stuff into the neck cavity of the turkey.

Sauces

Bread Sauce (serves 6–8)

You can make your bread sauce several days beforehand and store it in a covered container in the fridge, stirring in the cream when you reheat it.

1 onion
4–6 cloves
1 bay leaf
1 pt (500 ml) milk
3–4 (75–100 g) fresh white breadcrumbs
2 oz (50 g) butter
2–3 gratings of a whole nutmeg
salt, black pepper
a little cream or top of the milk

Peel the onion and stick the cloves into it. Put the onion, bay leaf and milk in a pan and bring to the boil. Remove from heat, cover pan and leave for 20–30 minutes. Add the breadcrumbs and butter. Cook the sauce uncovered, over the lowest possible heat (I use an asbestos mat) for 15–20 minutes and then remove the onion and bay leaf. Season to taste with nutmeg, salt, and freshly ground black pepper. Stir in a little cream before serving.

Spiced Cranberry and Orange Sauce (serves 6–8)
3oz (75 g) granulated sugar
5 fl oz (125 ml) fresh orange juice
6 oz (150 g) fresh cranberries
½ teaspoon (2.5 ml spoon) cinnamon *and* ½ teaspoon nutmeg
or 1 teaspoon (5 ml spoon) ground allspice

Stir the sugar into the orange juice in a pan and add the cranberries and spice. Cover, bring to the boil and simmer for 5 minutes. Store in a covered container in the fridge.

Roast Potatoes and Vegetables

Potatoes can be one of the best parts of the meal or one of the most boring. Perfect crispy roast potatoes are wonderful but particularly difficult to achieve if you only have one oven in which you are cooking the turkey at length at a low heat. However, with a little forethought, it is possible. The day before, peel your potatoes, cut them up into smaller pieces than you normally would and boil them until completely cooked. Before you begin to roast the turkey turn the oven to Gas Mark 9/475°F/240°C. Melt lots of good dripping in a large roasting pan so that it is about 1 in. (2 cm) deep. When the fat is smoking put in the boiled potatoes and spoon the fat all over them. Put them right at the top of the oven for 20–30 minutes until they are beginning to brown and crisp. Now turn the oven down to Gas Mark 3/325°F/160°C ready for the turkey. Put the turkey in below the potatoes. Turn the potatoes once or twice while the turkey is cooking – they should get beautifully brown and crispy all over, but roast potatoes are a bit like pastry – you are never quite sure how they'll turn out. When they look perfectly brown move them to the bottom of the oven below the turkey.

All I can say about your vegetables is: don't overcook them. I think it is much more important to cook one vegetable perfectly, rather than several badly because you are too busy. I buy the smallest sprouts I can find, prepare them the day before – but cook at the last moment for 5–6 minutes only so that they are still slightly crisp and bright green. It is now possible to buy circular steamers which expand or contract to fit any size saucepan. Vegetables cooked in this simple way taste much better and the goodness doesn't seep away into the water.

Broad Beans and Almonds in Chive Cream

Serves 6

If you are tired of having Brussels sprouts with your turkey every Christmas or want an extra vegetable which doesn't take long to prepare, try this mixture.

1 lb (400 g) frozen broad beans
3–4 oz (75–100 g) whole blanched almonds
a good knob of butter
1 carton fresh soured cream
2 rounded teaspoons (2 × 5 ml spoon) dried chives

Boil the broad beans in salted water until cooked. Drain, put into a serving dish with the almonds and dot with butter. Stir the chives into the soured cream and spoon it over the broad beans. Cover the dish and keep warm until you eat, giving it a stir just before you start so that the cream coats the beans and nuts well.

Our Favourite Christmas Pudding

Makes 2 puddings, each feeding 8–10 people

This is an old North Country recipe for a dark, moist full-flavoured pudding. I make it every year and it seems to have just the right mature, traditional flavour.

4 oz (100 g) self-raising flour
½ teaspoon (2.5 ml spoon) salt
1 teaspoon (5 ml spoon) mixed spice
1 teaspoon (5 ml spoon) ground cinnamon
½–¾ of a whole nutmeg – grated
½ teaspoon (2.5 ml spoon) ground cloves
8 oz (200 g) shredded suet
10 oz (250 g) fresh white breadcrumbs
grated rind and juice of 1 lemon and 1 orange
½ lb (200 g) demerara sugar
½ lb (200 g) grated carrots
½ lb (200 g) grated cooking apples
12 oz (300 g) raisins
8 oz (200 g) currants
8 oz (200 g) sultanas
4 oz (100 g) mixed peel
2 oz (50 g) flaked almonds
2 tablespoons (2 × 15 ml spoon) black treacle
½ large wineglass Cointreau or brandy
4 lightly whisked eggs (size 4)

Sieve the flour, salt and spice into a large mixing bowl. Add all the remaining dry ingredients. Mix together thoroughly. Melt the treacle in a pan to make it a little runny. Stir into it the lemon and orange juice and the Cointreau or brandy and finally the eggs. Pour the liquid into the pudding mixture and stir thoroughly. Cover the bowl with a cloth and leave until the next day. Butter two 2-pt pudding basins and spoon in the mixture. Cover with a double layer of buttered greaseproof paper and then either a cloth tied on with string or foil tucked in round the rim. Steam for 5–6 hours in pans of simmering water which should be kept topped up two-thirds up the sides of the basins. When cool, re-cover the basins and store in a cool place. On Christmas Day steam for a further 2–3 hours.

Rum Butter

Serves 6–8

When I was a child and didn't like Christmas pudding very much the only reason I would eat a spoonful was to have a huge dollop of rum or brandy butter on the top. Now my children feel the same. If you prefer brandy butter make it with icing sugar and brandy. You can make the butter when you make the pudding, pack it into a plastic box with a lid and store it in your refrigerator. Take out well beforehand on Christmas Day.

8 oz (200 g) unsalted butter
4–6 oz (100–150 g) (to taste) soft, pale brown sugar
4–5 tablespoons (4–5 × 15 ml spoon) light rum

Cream the butter until pale and soft. Beat in the sugar. Add the rum drop by drop, beating all the time so that it doesn't curdle.

Our Favourite Christmas Pudding with Rum Butter

Chocolate Crunch Christmas Pudding

Serves 8–10

If you are not insistent on sticking to tradition you can make this, which is not a Christmas pudding at all (it is crunchy and cold instead of soft and hot) but it looks perfect as an alternative on Christmas Day. It also has the advantage of being extremely quick to make and is much more popular than Christmas pudding with most children, and several adults too. It is expensive on chocolate but rich and filling and goes a long way.

For the pudding
6 oz (150 g) butter or margarine
3 tablespoons (3 × 15 ml spoon) golden syrup
8 oz (200 g) plain chocolate
6 oz (150 g) crushed ginger biscuits
6 oz (150 g) crushed plain sweet biscuits
1 oz (25 g) currants
3 oz (75 g) raisins
2 oz (50 g) glacé cherries – roughly chopped
1 oz (25 g) candied peel
2 teaspoons (2 × 5 ml spoon) ground cinnamon
2 tablespoons (2 × 15 ml spoon) brandy or rum

For the icing and decoration
3 oz (75 g) plain chocolate
1 tablespoon (15 ml spoon) water
1 oz (25 g) butter or margarine
a little icing sugar, 2–3 halved glacé cherries and a sprig of holly for decoration

Grease a 2-pt pudding basin. Gently melt and stir together the butter, syrup and chocolate in a saucepan. Mix in the rest of the ingredients and spoon into the pudding basin. Chill in the refrigerator until set. Then dip the basin briefly in hot water and turn the pudding out.

To make the icing, gently melt the chocolate with the water and stir until smooth, add the butter and stir until melted in. Cool very slightly and then ice the pudding all over with the chocolate. When cold, sprinkle a little icing sugar over the top of the pudding (to look like a sprinkling of snow!), stick in the sprig of holly and press the glacé cherries in a cluster round it. Keep in a cool place, but not in the fridge. Serve, with cream, cut into slices with a sharp knife.

Chilled Brandy Sauce

Serves 6–8

This quickly made, light and creamy sauce is an alternative to rum or brandy butter with the Christmas pudding – in fact, it's delicious with almost any hot pudding.

$\frac{1}{4}$ pt (125 ml) double cream
1 level tablespoon (15 ml spoon) icing sugar – sifted
1–2 tablespoons (1–2 × 15 ml spoon) brandy

Simply whisk the cream until thick, then whisk in the icing sugar and gradually stir in the brandy to taste. Chill in the refrigerator.

First Courses and Snacks

I have given up having a first course to the Christmas dinner since it's always such a noisy and chaotic meal, with the over-excitement of the children and the table covered with decorations and crackers, not to mention many dishes of food. A first course just over-complicates things and everyone has far too much to eat anyway. However, eating leads to more eating and my family's appetites seem to double during those few festive days. The following dishes are useful at other meals, for friends dropping in or for a lighter lunch or supper.

Chicken Liver and Almond Pâté

Serves 6–8

Chicken liver pâté is one of the easiest to make, but I have always found the taste slightly strong and the texture a little smooth. However, this is a mild version in which the orange juice and cream soften the strong liver taste and the chopped almonds give a crunchiness to the texture. If you are not using it in a stuffing you can use the liver from your turkey in this recipe.

4 oz (100 g) unsalted butter
1 small onion – chopped finely
8 oz (200 g) chicken livers
1 rounded teaspoon mild French mustard
1 level teaspoon (5 ml spoon) ground nutmeg
salt, black pepper
2 tablespoons (2 × 15 ml spoon) brandy
juice of ½ orange
2 tablespoons (2 × 15 ml spoon) cream
1 oz (25 g) chopped blanched almonds
1 teaspoon (5 ml spoon) fresh or dried chives (optional)

Melt 1 oz (25 g) butter in a frying pan and gently cook the onion until soft. Add the chicken livers and cook gently, stirring once or twice for 5 minutes. Add the mustard and nutmeg, a further 2 oz (50 g) butter, salt and pepper. When the butter has melted, remove from the heat and add the brandy, orange juice and cream. Whizz up in a liquidiser until smooth, or press through a sieve. Stir the chopped almonds into the mixture and all but a sprinkling of the chives. Transfer to an earthenware dish and sprinkle top with the remaining chives.

Gently bubble the remaining 1 oz (25 g) butter in a pan for a minute. Remove from the heat and let stand for another minute or two. Then pour the melted butter through a fine sieve or coffee strainer over the top of the pâté. Let cool. Then cover with foil and chill well in the fridge before serving with thin toast.

Layered Sardine Loaf

Serves 8–10

This unusual fish pâté has every advantage. Firstly, it is delicious. It is easy to make and inexpensive. It freezes well or can be made and chilled in the fridge a day in advance. Lastly, with its dark green parsley and butter top, it has an extremely impressive appearance. It is perfect either as a first course or as an accompaniment to cold meats.

4 oz (100 g) butter or block margarine
1 lb (400 g) cream cheese – at room temperature
2 tins sardines
juice of ½ lemon
2–3 cloves garlic – crushed or chopped finely
salt, black pepper
good handful of parsley – chopped finely
approx. 1 small loaf wholemeal or granary bread – sliced thinly

Butter a loaf tin, size about 9 in. × 5 in. (23 cm × 13 cm). Melt 3 oz (75 g) butter and leave it to cool a bit. Put in the cream cheese in a mixing bowl and mash the sardines into it with a wooden spoon. Stir in the lemon juice, garlic and melted butter bit by bit. Add salt and plenty of black pepper. Mix all together thoroughly. Melt the remaining 1 oz (25 g) butter and stir into it the chopped parsley. Spread this mixture on the bottom of the loaf tin. Cut the rinds off the slices of bread and cut to shape to make a layer of bread on top of the parsley, then spread a rather thick layer of the cream cheese mixture over the bread, then another layer of bread, and so on, ending with a layer of bread. Cover with foil or plastic film and chill overnight in the fridge.

To turn out, dip the tin briefly in hot water and slip the loaf on to a serving dish. If necessary smooth the sides with a knife. Chill again in the fridge until needed.

Layered Sardine Loaf

Featherlight Cheese Biscuits

The adults can nibble these with their Christmas drinks and the children, who love making them, can just nibble them! They will keep crisp in an airtight tin.

6 oz (150 g) grated cheese
4 oz (100 g) plain wholemeal flour
2 level teaspoons (2 × 5 ml spoon) baking powder
2 teaspoons (2 × 5 ml spoon) paprika (or variations – either 1 rounded teaspoon (2 × 5 ml spoon) curry powder or 1 level teaspoon (5 ml spoon) caraway seeds)
4 oz (100 g) butter or margarine
2 egg yolks

Preheat oven to Gas Mark 7/425°F/220°C. Put the grated cheese into a mixing bowl. Sift the flour with the baking powder and paprika into the cheese. Cut the butter into small pieces and rub into the flour and cheese with your fingertips. Add the egg yolks and mix with a wooden spoon to a stiff dough. Gather into a ball, press out with your hands on a floured board and roll out to about ½ in. (1 cm) thick. Cut into small biscuits with a 2 in. (5 cm) cutter or the rim of a glass. Place on a large ungreased baking sheet. Bake at the top of the oven for 8–12 minutes until light golden brown. Cool before removing from the baking sheet.

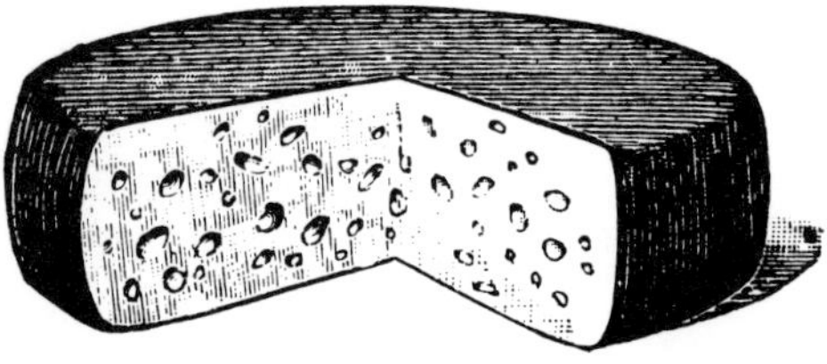

Stuffed Cheese Shortbread

As a snack or to liven up a leftovers meal of bits and pieces these light, crunchy biscuits, combined with a creamy cheese and chive mixture, are very tempting. You can make the biscuits days before and keep them in an airtight tin until you need them, and of course you can eat them just on their own.

For the biscuits
6 oz (150 g) plain flour
1 teaspoon (5 ml spoon) salt
3 oz (75 g) fine semolina
For the spread
4 oz (100 g) strong cheddar cheese – grated finely
6 oz (150 g) butter – at room temperature
6 oz (150 g) cream cheese
1 tablespoon (15 ml spoon) chopped dried chives or spring onions
black pepper

Heat oven to Gas Mark 2/300°F/150°C. Lightly grease a large baking sheet or tin. Mix the flour, salt and semolina together in a bowl. Add the cheese and butter. Work the mixture together thoroughly with your fingers until you have a smooth dough. Roll out thickly – about ½ in. (1 cm) – on a floured board and cut into small biscuits with a 2 in. (5 cm) cutter or the rim of a glass. Arrange on the baking sheet and bake in the centre of the oven for 1 hour. Allow to cool a little and then transfer the biscuits to a wire tray to cool completely.

To make the cream cheese mixture, simply soften the cream cheese with a fork and mix in the chopped chives and black pepper to taste. Use either to sandwich together the biscuits or just to spread on top of them.

Creamy Aubergine Purée

Serves 6

This most delicious cold purée from Turkey is deceptively easy to make and aubergines are plentiful in the shops during the winter. It is very light in texture and has a distinctive smoky taste. Serve it as a first course with toast, as a dip at a buffet or simply as a snack.

2 medium-size aubergines
juice of ½ lemon
approx 3 tablespoons (3 × 15 ml spoon) sunflower oil
salt, black pepper
a little chopped parsley to garnish

Put the aubergines, unpeeled, under a very hot grill, turning them once or twice until the skin is black and beginning to blister. This will probably take 15–25 minutes. Now peel off all the skin. As they will be hot this is easier to do under cold water. Put them in a large sieve and press them down with a wooden spoon or a plate so that as much juice as possible comes out of them. They will now look like old rags, but don't worry, a miraculous transformation is about to take place! Put them into the liquidiser with the lemon juice. Whizz up and add the sunflower oil a little at a time until the mixture is smooth, pale and very light. The more oil you add, the lighter the texture.

Add salt and pepper to taste. Store in a covered plastic dish in the fridge for up to a week, or freeze. To serve, spoon into a bowl and sprinkle on a little chopped parsley.

Creamy Aubergine Purée and Stuffed Cheese Shortbread

Kipper and Onion Quiche with Cheese Pastry

Serves 6–8

A good quiche is always popular and this one, made with kipper fillets, is a tasty contrast to all the meat and turkey one eats at Christmas time. You can make the quiche in advance – it freezes well. Warmed up and accompanied simply by a crisp green salad it makes an effortless supper dish on Christmas Eve.

For a change, replace kippers with smoked mackerel fillets.

For the pastry
10 oz (250 g) plain flour
good pinch of salt
5 oz (125 g) butter or margarine
2 oz (50 g) lard
3 oz (75 g) grated cheese
1 lightly whisked egg (size 3)
For the filling
3 eggs and 1 extra yolk (size 3)
approx. ¼ pt (125 ml) single cream or milk
salt, black pepper
2 large onions
1 oz (25 g) butter or margarine for frying
2–3 (according to size) kipper fillets

Sift the flour and salt into a mixing bowl. Cut the butter and lard into the flour and rub with your fingertips until it is like breadcrumbs. Stir in the grated cheese with a knife, then the egg and a very little cold water until the mixture just sticks together. Gather into a ball, wrap in foil and cool in the fridge for at least half an hour. Then roll the pastry on a floured board and line a buttered 9 in. (23 cm) flan dish with it. Prick the base of the pastry lightly with a fork.

To make the filling, whisk the eggs lightly and mix in a bowl with the cream, salt and black pepper. Chop the onions into small pieces and fry gently in butter or margarine until soft and transparent. Scrape the kipper flesh from the skin, remove any bones and flake it into the cream-and-egg mixture. Stir in the fried onion. Pour the mixture into the pastry case and bake in the centre of a preheated oven at Gas Mark 5/375°F/190°C for 30–40 minutes until just firm in the centre.

Smoked Fish and Almond Mousse

Serves 6–8

This light mousse is topped with crisp almond flakes. It makes a good contrast to the Christmas meat and turkey, either as a first course or eaten with the cold meats. It is easy to make if you have a liquidiser, and you can either freeze it or make it a day or two beforehand. It should be served well chilled.

1 lb (400 g) smoked cod or whiting fillets
2 lightly whisked eggs
3 tablespoons (3 × 15 ml spoon) milk
juice of ½ lemon
1 oz (25 g) butter
2 oz (50 g) flaked almonds
½ pt (250 ml) double cream
2 teaspoons (2 × 5 ml spoon) dried fennel, oregano or tarragon
salt, black pepper

Heat oven to Gas Mark 4/350°F/180°C. Put a roasting pan full of hot water on the centre shelf. Chop the fish roughly and remove any skin. Drop the eggs and milk into the liquidiser. Add about a quarter of the fish and whizz up until smooth and then add the lemon juice and the rest of the fish bit by bit, whizzing after each addition. As it gets very thick you will probably have to stop and stir it around now and then to make sure it all turns to a smooth purée. Transfer to a bowl. Melt the butter in a pan and quickly stir the flaked almonds around it until well coated. Remove from heat. Whisk up the cream until fairly thick, not stiff, and stir gently into the fish purée. Season with herbs, a little salt and plenty of black pepper.

Butter a soufflé dish and spoon the mixture into it. Smooth top and sprinkle with the butter-coated almonds. Put the dish in the pan of water in the oven and cook for 25–30 minutes. Leave to cool and chill well before serving.

Hot Main Dishes

If your family arrive on Christmas Eve it's nice to have a dish which prepares their taste buds for the treats in store and which will put them in a festive mood. Through the holiday you may need one or two good hot dishes which contrast well with the other Christmas tastes, and after one or two meals of eating up the cold turkey and meats a sizzling hot dish becomes very welcome again.

Roast Pork with Tomato and Tarragon Sauce

Serves 6–8

If you like to have a joint of pork at Christmas, it can be enormously enhanced by an interesting sauce instead of the usual brown gravy. This rich tomato sauce is no trouble to make but adds greatly to the succulence and flavour of the meat.

1 3–4 lb (1.2–1.6 kg) joint pork on the bone
3–4 cloves garlic – chopped finely
juice of 1 lemon
sunflower or groundnut oil
salt, black pepper
For the sauce
1 tin tomatoes
1 large glass red wine
2 teaspoons (2 × 5 ml spoon) French mustard
1 teaspoon (5 ml spoon) sugar
2 teaspoons (2 × 5 ml spoon) dried tarragon
juices from the meat
1 dessertspoon (10 ml spoon) cornflour
salt, black pepper

Make deep incisions in the meat and poke the chopped garlic in as far as you can. If not already done by the butcher, score the thick fat closely with a sharp knife. Mix the lemon juice and twice as much oil with salt and black pepper in a cup and smear all over the meat. Put the joint in a roasting pan and if possible cover the meat with foil. Leave for at least two hours at room temperature, spooning the juices over the meat again once or twice.

Heat the oven to Gas Mark 9/475°F/240°C. Remove foil from the meat. Rub the scored fat with salt and a little extra oil (this should produce golden crisp crackling) and roast at the high heat for 20 minutes, then turn down the oven to Gas Mark 3/325°F/160°C and cook for a further 2–2¼ hours.

Before the meat is quite ready, put the tomatoes, wine, mustard, sugar and tarragon into a saucepan. Blend the cornflour until smooth with a little water and add to the mixture. Bring to the boil, stirring, and bubble for 2–3 minutes. Add salt and black pepper to taste.

When the meat is ready, pour the excess fat from the pan and add the meat juices to the sauce. If the sauce seems too thick add a little more wine or water. Pour the sauce into a serving jug and pour over the meat when carved.

Red Velvet Casserole of Beef

Serves 6–8

A precooked casserole is useful to have ready over Christmas to heat up when everyone is tired of cold turkey. This flavourful beef, wrapped thickly in a smooth red sauce, looks particularly festive.

rind and juice of 1 large orange
1 lb (400 g) cooked beetroot
1 level tablespoon (15 ml spoon) sugar
2–3 cloves garlic
½ pt (250 ml) water
1¾–2 lb (700–800 g) best stewing steak
1 oz (25 g) butter
2 tablespoons (2 × 15 ml spoon) olive or sunflower oil
2 rounded teaspoons (4 × 5 ml spoon) ground ginger
1 rounded tablespoon (2 × 15 ml spoon) plain flour
salt, black pepper
1 carton fresh soured cream

Grate the orange rind. Roughly chop the beetroot and put into a liquidiser with the orange juice, orange rind, sugar, garlic and water. Whizz to a smooth purée. You may need to do this quantity in two goes. Cut up the stewing steak into largish slices. Melt the butter and oil together in an iron-based casserole on top of the stove or in a large saucepan. Stir the meat into the melted fat and sprinkle on the ground ginger. Remove from heat and stir in a level tablespoonful of plain flour. Heat the beetroot purée and stir into the beef. If you are already using a casserole put on the lid and cook in a preheated oven at Gas Mark 1/275°F/140°C for 2–2½ hours or until the beef is tender (if you started in a saucepan transfer the mixture to a casserole). Check for seasoning and add salt and pepper.

Just before serving, spoon the soured cream over the top. Serve with baked potatoes or rice and a green vegetable or salad.

Red Velvet Casserole of Beef

Duck with Gooseberry and Brazil Nut Stuffing

Serves 4–6

If you are a small family and decide to have duck at Christmas, this gooseberry and nut stuffing and sauce makes a nice change from the traditional orange sauce. Made in a slightly larger quantity it is also good for goose.

1 $4\frac{1}{2}$–$5\frac{1}{2}$ lb (1.75–2.25 kg) duck
For the stuffing
2 oz (50 g) pearl barley
coarsely grated rind and juice of 1 small orange
drained gooseberries from 1 small tin
heart and liver of the duck – chopped finely
2 oz (50 g) brazil nuts – chopped finely
2 oz (50 g) melted butter
1 lightly whisked egg (size 4)
salt, black pepper
For the sauce
juice from the tin of gooseberries
1 small glass sweet vermouth or sherry
juices from the duck
approx. 2 level teaspoons (2 × 5 ml spoon) arrowroot or cornflour
salt, black pepper

Boil the pearl barley in unsalted water, until tender but still slightly nutty. Rinse through with cold water and then mix thoroughly with the rest of the stuffing ingredients. Season well. Stuff the whole of the duck with this mixture and truss up or stick skewers in to keep down the loose skin of the neck and hold the legs together. Heat oven to Gas Mark 6/400°F/200°C. Rub a little salt all over the skin of the duck and roast in the centre of the oven, first on one side for 30 minutes then the other side for 30 minutes and finally on its back for 40–50 minutes.

Transfer the duck to a serving plate and keep warm. Then pour off the fat from the juices (keep the fat, as it is wonderful for fried and roast potatoes) and pour the juices into a saucepan. Add the gooseberry juice and vermouth. Blend the arrowroot (this will make a transparent, shiny sauce) or cornflour with a little water and stir into the juices. Bring to the boil and bubble, stirring, for 2–3 minutes. Season with salt and pepper. Serve in a sauce jug with the duck. Don't forget to spoon all the delicious stuffing out.

Turkey au Gratin with Almonds

Serves 6

This is one easy way to make your scraps of cold turkey into a deliciously satisfying hot dish. You can make it in a quiet moment and reheat it, or you can keep it hot in a low oven for hours.

For the meat
approx. 2 lb (800 g) cooked, boneless turkey
4 oz (100 g) blanched almonds – whole or split
1 oz (25 g) butter or margarine
For the sauce
2–3 oz (50–75 g) butter or margarine
2 heaped tablespoons (2 × 15 ml spoon) plain flour
1¼ pts (625 ml) milk
½ small glass sherry
6 oz (150 g) grated cheese
2 large cloves garlic – crushed
a little grated parmesan cheese
salt, black pepper
chopped parsley for decoration

Heat the oven to Gas Mark 3/325°F/160°C. Cut the turkey into pieces and arrange in a large, fairly shallow, oven-proof dish. Melt the 1 oz (25 g) butter in a frying pan and toss the almonds in it for a minute or two until golden brown. Sprinkle them over the cold turkey.

To make the sauce, melt the butter in a fairly large saucepan, take off the heat and stir in the flour with a wooden spoon. Gradually stir in the milk and bring to the boil, stirring all the time until it is a thick and smooth white sauce. Let it simmer, still stirring, for 2–3 minutes. Then add the sherry, grated cheese, garlic, salt and black pepper and stir until the cheese has melted.

Pour the sauce over the turkey and almonds. Dot with butter and sprinkle with the grated parmesan. Cook in the centre of the oven for 30–45 minutes until golden brown.

Before serving, sprinkle chopped parsley round the edges of the dish. Serve with a salad.

Turkey au Gratin with Almonds

Spicy Beef and Guinness Pie

Serves 6–8

A golden pie which looks and tastes extra-special. It is most suitable for one of your festive meals as it can be prepared well beforehand and will only need putting into the oven to bake. If you have an aversion to prunes don't be put off – they disintegrate in the stout and produce the most delicious, rich, dark sauce. The juniper berries are optional but can be found in most delicatessens and will add tantalisingly to the flavour. Allspice is best ground from whole berries but you can also buy it ground (just to muddle you it is sometimes known as Pimento or Jamaica pepper). If you can't find allspice use more nutmeg and two more cloves. For the top you can use packet puff pastry if you like but the easy flaky pastry is very little trouble and beautifully crisp. Make your pastry first or while the pie filling is cooking.

For the easy flaky pastry
8 oz (200 g) plain flour
good pinch salt
6 oz (150 g) from an 8 oz block frozen butter or margarine
6 tablespoons (6 × 15 ml spoon) very cold water – preferably chilled in the fridge
For the glaze – 1 egg yolk

For the pie filling
1 teaspoon (5 ml spoon) whole allspice berries
6 cloves
1 teaspoon (5 ml spoon) juniper berries (optional)
1 tablespoon (15 ml spoon) oil
$\frac{1}{4}$–$\frac{1}{2}$ whole nutmeg – grated
2–3 large cloves garlic – chopped finely
2 lb (800 g) lean stewing beef – chopped in cubes
$\frac{1}{2}$ pt bottle Guinness or other stout
8 oz (200 g) large prunes – soaked in water overnight
1 lb (400 g) carrots – cleaned and sliced
salt, black pepper
2 teaspoons (2 × 5 ml spoon) arrowroot

To make the pastry, sift the flour and salt into a bowl. Put a grater into the bowl on top of the flour. Hold the frozen butter in its wrapping and coarsely grate off 6 oz (three-quarters of the block). With a palette knife mix the fat into the flour until crumbly. Now add the water gradually, mixing again with the knife and then gather the dough up with your hands into a ball. Wrap in foil or polythene and put in the fridge for at least an hour.

Heat the oven to Gas Mark 1/275°F/140°C. Crush the allspice and cloves together in a pestle and mortar or in a coffee grinder, add the juniper berries and crush roughly. Heat the oil in the bottom of an iron casserole. Put the crushed spices together with the grated nutmeg and chopped garlic into the hot oil and stir over the heat for ½ minute. Add the beef and just seal all over for 2–3 minutes over a high heat. Stir in the stout and ½ cup water. Remove the stones from the soaked prunes and add. Bring to the boil and then cover the dish and cook in the oven at Gas Mark 1/275°F/140°C for an hour. (Make the pastry now if you haven't already.) Then add the carrots and continue cooking for a further 1–1½ hours until the meat is tender. Season to taste with salt and black pepper. Blend the arrowroot with a spot of water and stir in. Bubble for a minute or two on top of the stove. Then pour into a 2½-pt pie dish and leave until cold.

When the filling is cold, roll out the pastry on a floured surface to roughly the size and shape of the pie dish. Moisten the edge of the dish and lay the pastry on top. Cut round the edges and press down lightly. Roll out the trimmings and use to make a pattern, or cut-out letters to read "Happy Christmas"! Cover the pastry loosely with plastic film or foil and put the complete dish in the fridge until the next day, or in the freezer (if the freezer, remember to defrost before baking).

To bake, heat the oven to Gas Mark 7/425°F/220°C. Brush the pastry all over with egg yolk and cook in the centre of the oven for about 20 minutes until a rich golden brown. Serve with a green salad.

Spicy Beef and Guinness Pie

The Cold Table and Salads

It is useful to have cold meat around over Christmas but it must be full of flavour to contrast with the blandness of the cold turkey.

Good salads, also, are essential at Christmas to accompany cold meats and turkey or to go with ready-prepared hot dishes so that you won't have to be busy cooking vegetables at the last minute. I have included a few less usual salads which can be prepared and most of them dressed beforehand without losing their fresh appearance and taste.

"In a sallet every plant should come in to bear its part without being overpowered by some herb of a stronger taste, but fall into their places like the notes in music".

John Evelyn (1620–1706)

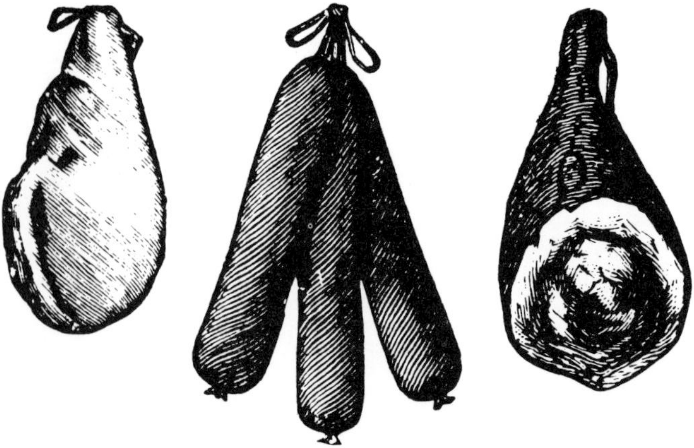

Treacle Baked Collar of Bacon

Serves 8–12

This aromatic piece of meat will keep well, foil-wrapped in the fridge. It is ideal for a party or if you are feeding a lot of people over Christmas. You can cook any bacon or gammon joint in this way but collar is an economical cut. You can use smoked or green bacon, but I nearly always go for smoked meat because I prefer the flavour.

$2\frac{1}{2}$–3 lb (1–1.25 kg) piece of collar of bacon
$\frac{1}{4}$ oz ($\frac{1}{2} \times 2.5$ ml spoon) allspice berries *and* $\frac{1}{4}$ oz cloves *or* just $\frac{1}{2}$ oz (2.5 ml spoon) cloves
$\frac{1}{4}$–$\frac{1}{2}$ oz ($\frac{1}{2}$–1×2.5 ml spoon) black peppercorns
black treacle
demerara sugar

Soak the bacon in cold water for at least 3 hours or overnight, changing the water once or twice, to remove excess saltiness. Put the spices and peppercorns into a liquidiser or coffee grinder and whizz up until roughly ground. Mix them with enough black treacle to smear thickly all over the bacon joint. Wrap up well in two or three layers of foil. Put into a roasting pan and cook in a low oven at Gas Mark 1/275°F/140°C for 3–4 hours, according to size. Remove from the oven, unwrap, cut off the thick bacon skin while still hot and pour off any juices. Wrap again in foil, put heavy books or weights on top and leave to cool for 12 hours or overnight.

Then chill in the fridge and when you unwrap the foil sprinkle demerara sugar thickly all over the fat where the skin was taken off. As with most cold meats, this is most delicious if carved as thinly as possible.

Honey Pork with Raisin and Rosemary Stuffing

Serves 6–8

Cold roast pork can be rather dry and dull. This way of stuffing it and cooking it in honey makes the joint particularly moist and full of flavour, while its glossy appearance is festive and inviting.

1–2 sprigs rosemary or 2 teaspoons (2 × 5 ml spoon) dried rosemary
3–4 oz (75–100 g) seedless raisins
1–2 cloves garlic
$2\frac{1}{2}$–$3\frac{1}{2}$ lb (1–1.5 kg) rolled pork shoulder or belly
salt, black pepper
approx. 2 tablespoons (2 × 15 ml spoon) honey

Take the leaves off the rosemary sprigs and chop them up finely with the raisins and garlic. Press this mixture deep into the gaps in the meat or, if the meat hasn't been rolled yet by the butcher, spread the stuffing on, then roll up and tie securely with string. Sprinkle all over with salt and pepper. Then press the honey in with the raisin mixture and smear honey liberally all over the joint including the hard skin and fat, which should be scored first with a sharp knife. Put the meat on a piece of foil in a roasting pan. Bring the foil up round the joint, to keep the honey juices close around the meat, but leaving the hard skin on top exposed. Put on a high shelf in the oven at Gas Mark 7/425°F/220°C for 10 minutes until the top is turning golden brown. Then baste with the honey juices and bring the meat down on to a lower shelf. Turn down the oven to Gas Mark 3/325°F/160°C and cook, basting occasionally, for a further 2–$2\frac{1}{2}$ hours.

Put the meat on a plate to cool. Reserve the juices but pour off the excess fat. Put the juices in a pan and bubble fiercely for a minute or two until thickened. Brush this glaze all over the meat and then leave to become completely cold. Keep in the fridge and carve thinly.

Honey Pork with Raisin and Rosemary Stuffing

Herring and Apple in Soured Cream

Serves 4

This delicious concoction only takes minutes to prepare, so eat it the same day when the apples are still crunchy. It is perfect as a first course or as a more interesting accompaniment to cold meat and salad.

2–3 (5–6 oz, 125–150 g) pickled herring fillets
1 carton fresh soured cream
1 medium size cooking apple – peeled and cut in small, thin pieces
1 small onion – sliced finely
½ teaspoon (2.5 ml spoon) grated or ground nutmeg
salt, black pepper
a little parsley to garnish

Rinse the fillets thoroughly under cold water, pat dry and cut them into small pieces. Mix in a bowl with the cream, apple, onion and nutmeg, adding salt and pepper to taste. Transfer the mixture to a serving dish and sprinkle with chopped parsley. Serve with thin slices of brown bread.

Country Veal Terrine

Serves 18–20

This large terrine, turned out of its dish, neatly striped with bacon and glossy with its own delicious jelly, is a beautiful sight at a Christmas party, and although it is straightforward to do you are bound to feel triumphant! It can be made well in advance and kept in the fridge for up to two weeks. If you are unable to get veal you can use lean pork or even boned chicken instead.

For the marinade
1–1½ glasses sherry
1 heaped tablespoon (2 × 15 ml spoon) soft brown sugar
10 crushed allspice *or* juniper berries
approx. 8 peppercorns
1 heaped tablespoon (2 × 15 ml spoon) finely chopped sage
approx. 4 bay leaves
2–3 teaspoons (2–3 × 5 ml spoon) mixed spice
2 teaspoons (2 × 5 ml spoon) ground mace or nutmeg
plenty of salt and black pepper
For the terrine
1½ lb (600 g) pie veal
1 lb (400 g) belly of pork
¾ lb (300 g) pig's liver
(minced through the coarse blade of a mincer)
¾ lb (300 g) thinly sliced smoked streaky bacon
4–5 black peppercorns *or* whole juniper berries

Mix the marinade ingredients together in a large dish. Mix the minced veal, belly of pork and pig's liver into the marinade mixture. Cover and leave for about 8 hours at room temperature.

Grease a 2-pt earthenware dish. Remove the bay leaves from the marinade and arrange on the bottom of the dish in a pattern with four or five peppercorns or juniper berries. Lay the bacon neatly in strips on the bottom and sides of the dish, reserving enough to lay on top of the terrine. Spoon the meat and marinade mixture into the dish. Lay the remaining strips of bacon on the top. Cover with greased foil and then a lid and put the dish in a pan of water in the oven at Gas Mark 3/325°F/160°C for $1\frac{1}{2}$–2 hours or until it starts to shrink away from the sides. Cool for half an hour, then put a board and some weights or books on top of the dish (try to reserve any juice that spills over the sides) and leave for an hour or two.

Remove board and weights and chill in the fridge. The easiest way to turn the terrine on to a serving dish is to dip the dish in very hot water up to the rim for about half a minute or just until the terrine flops out when you turn it upside down and give it a good shake.

Melt any reserved jelly juices and brush the top of the terrine with them. Return to the fridge until you serve it.

Country Veal Terrine

Red Cabbage, Parsnip and Hazelnut Salad

Serves 8

The subtle, sweet flavour of the parsnip is an important part of this excellent winter salad.

For the salad
1 medium-size red cabbage
½ lb (200 g) small parsnips – boiled and cut in quarters
2–3 oz (50–75 g) hazelnuts
1 dessertspoon (10 ml spoon) dried fennel or tarragon
For the French dressing
3 tablespoons (3 × 15 ml spoon) red wine vinegar
6 tablespoons (6 × 15 ml spoon) olive oil
1 teaspoon (5 ml spoon) soft brown sugar
1 crushed clove garlic (optional)
salt, black pepper

Simply slice the red cabbage very finely and mix in a bowl with the boiled parsnips and hazelnuts. Sprinkle over the dried fennel. I find the easiest way to mix the French dressing is to have a jam jar with a tight-fitting lid kept for the purpose so that you can vigorously shake the ingredients up together.

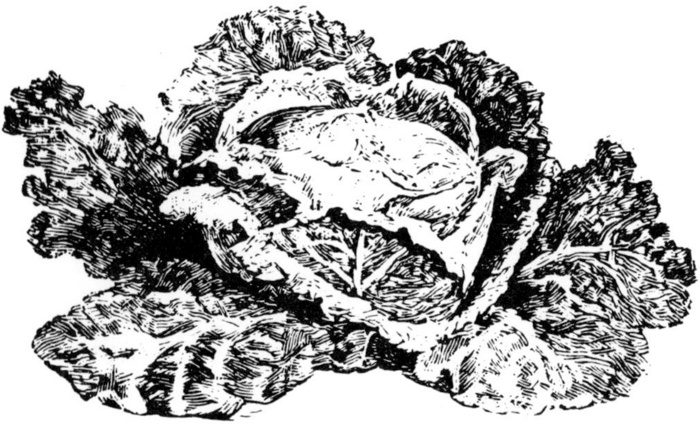

Parsnip Salad with Brazil Nuts

Serves 6–8

You may think cooked parsnips would make an unlikely salad but in fact their subtle, slightly sweet flavour is most successful.

1 lb (400 g) small parsnips
3–4 sticks celery – sliced across rather finely
2 oz (50 g) shelled brazil nuts – chopped roughly
1 oz (25 g) candied peel
3 teaspoons (3 × 5 ml spoon) dried fennel or a handful of parsley – finely chopped
French dressing with 2 teaspoons (2 × 5 ml spoon) French mustard added (see p.54)

Peel the parsnips and cut in quarters. Boil them in salted water (or better still, steam them) until just tender. Drain and cool. Then mix all the ingredients together in a salad bowl and dress. This is one of those salads which won't suffer if you dress it a little before you eat it.

White Cabbage Salad with Blue Cheese Dressing

Serves 8

1 medium-size white cabbage (or Chinese cabbage)
3–4 oz (75–100 g) piece of Danish blue cheese
1 carton fresh soured cream
pinch of grated nutmeg
a little top of the milk or single cream

Slice the white cabbage finely and put in a bowl. To make the dressing blend all the other ingredients together (you can do this in seconds with a liquidiser) adding enough top of the milk to give a coating consistency. Season to taste with salt and black pepper.

Walnut Stuffed Breast of Veal

Serves 8–12

This deliciously stuffed joint can be prepared beforehand and will be ready to pop in your oven to provide yet another very special meal over Christmas. Alternatively, you can eat the joint cold or use the stuffing recipe as one of the stuffings for the turkey.

2½–3 lb (1–1.4 kg) boned breast of veal
2 oz (50 g) fresh breadcrumbs
good handful of parsley – chopped finely
3–4 oz (75–100 g) walnuts – chopped small
1 teaspoon (5 ml spoon) dried thyme or oregano
2 cloves garlic – crushed
salt, black pepper
1 lightly whisked egg
oil

If the veal has already been rolled up and tied, cut the string and lay the meat flat. Into a mixing bowl put the breadcrumbs, chopped parsley, walnuts, thyme, garlic, salt and plenty of black pepper. Mix together and then mix in the egg. Spread this mixture and press down over the meat. Then roll up and tie together with string. Smear the joint all over with oil and rub a little salt on the fat on the top. Roast in the centre of the oven at Gas Mark 3/325°F/160°C for 2–2½ hours, basting occasionally.

Walnut Stuffed Breast of Veal

Bean Salad with Lemon and Mustard Dressing

Serves 8

Dried beans are so useful for winter salads. It is said that they cook better if you soak them in rainwater: I have tried this but can't say that I can notice a difference!

For the salad
$\frac{1}{2}$ lb (200 g) dried haricot or red kidney beans
$\frac{3}{4}$ lb (300 g) frozen French beans
1 large onion – chopped finely
1 red pepper – sliced thinly (optional)
For the dressing
juice of 1 lemon
4–5 tablespoons (4–5 × 15 ml spoon) olive oil
1 teaspoon (5 ml spoon) honey
2 teaspoons (2 × 5 ml spoon) mild French mustard
salt, black pepper

Soak the dried beans in cold water overnight. Boil in unsalted water until tender – about $\frac{1}{2}$–1 hour, but the cooking time depends on the age of the beans. Rinse with cold water and drain. Cook the French beans in boiling, salted water for 2–3 minutes – they should still be slightly crunchy. Drain and mix in a salad bowl with the haricot beans, chopped onion and red pepper.

Put the dressing ingredients into an empty jam jar with a lid and shake thoroughly. Pour over the salad and toss.

Egg, Mushroom and Pimento Salad

Serves 6

A satisfying salad which can also be used as a first course to a meal.

1 carton fresh soured cream
2 heaped tablespoons (4 × 15 ml spoon) mayonnaise
3–4 teaspoons (3–4 × 5 ml spoon) mild French mustard
½ level teaspoon (2.5 ml spoon) ground cinnamon
black pepper, salt
4 sliced hardboiled eggs
1 large green or red pimento – sliced very thinly
½ lb (200 g) mushrooms – sliced thinly
chopped parsley for garnish

In a large bowl mix together the cream and the mayonnaise until smooth. Add the mustard, cinnamon, salt and black pepper to taste. Stir in the prepared pimento and mushrooms and lastly the sliced eggs. Transfer the mixture to a serving bowl and decorate the edges with chopped parsley.

Old-fashioned Spiced Beef

Serves 6–8

A good piece of spiced beef is particularly appropriate at Christmas time. It has a subtle, mellow flavour and can be carved in paper-thin slices. Either buy prepared salt meat or salt your own, using a method to be found in any standard recipe book.

3–4 lb (1.25–1.5 kg) joint of boned, salt silverside or brisket
black pepper
soft dark brown sugar (Muscovado or Barbados)
1 level tablespoon (15 ml spoon) whole allspice berries
1 level tablespoon (15 ml spoon) juniper berries
approx. 1 dessertspoon (10 ml spoon) cloves

First soak the joint in cold water for 2–4 hours, changing the water once or twice. Sprinkle the joint generously with black pepper. Rub the brown sugar quite thickly all over the joint. Crush the allspice and juniper berries in a mortar, liquidiser or coffee grinder and press all over the joint and into any cracks. I usually make one or two incisions to get some spices right to the centre of the meat. Stick the cloves into the joint all over. Wrap the joint up very thoroughly in foil and place in a large ovenproof dish with a well fitting lid, or in a roasting pan with more foil on top. If possible leave like this at room temperature overnight.

Cook in the centre of the oven Gas Mark 1/275°F/140°C for about $3\frac{1}{2}$–$4\frac{1}{2}$ hours, according to the size of the joint. Take out, open the foil slightly to let the juices pour away and wrap the foil round the joint again. Then leave in a cool place with a board and books or weights on top until the next day.

Keep it in the fridge in foil until you want to carve it. Carve as thinly as possible. Wrap up any leftover piece in foil again and store in the fridge. If you have had cranberry sauce with your turkey, this goes very well with the beef.

Old-fashioned Spiced Beef

Potato and Mushroom Salad

Serves 6

This is another more substantial salad which goes especially well with cold meat.

For the salad
1 lb (400 g) small potatoes
8 oz (200 g) button mushrooms
large bunch parsley – finely chopped
For the dressing
2 tablespoons (2 × 15 ml spoon) mayonnaise – a good bought kind will do
3 tablespoons (3 × 15 ml spoon) plain yoghurt
1–2 teaspoons (1–2 × 5 ml spoon) mild French mustard
salt, black pepper

Scrape (don't peel) the potatoes and boil until done. Cool and then slice. Slice the mushrooms downwards, keeping the stalk on so that they are a flat mushroom shape. Put all into a bowl with the chopped parsley.

To make the dressing simply stir up the ingredients with a fork until smooth, adding a little salt and plenty of black pepper. Coat the salad ingredients with this mixture and keep in the fridge until needed.

Tomato and Sage Salad

Serves 4–6

During the summer tomato salads are incomparably improved by the addition of fresh basil, and chopped fresh mint is very good too. In mid-winter it is difficult to find fresh herbs, other than greenhouse parsley, but the sage bush struggles on without losing all its leaves.

1–1½ lb (400–600 g) sliced tomatoes
good handful fresh sage leaves
French dressing (see p. 54)

Get a good handful of leaves and chop them very finely before adding to a tomato salad. Dress with a French dressing just before serving.

Celery, Red Cabbage and Spring Onion Salad

Serves 8

If you can find them, fennel roots are even better than celery in this salad, but celery is specially good at this time of year.

1 bunch celery
1 small red cabbage
1–2 bunches spring onions
yoghurt and mustard dressing (see p. 62)

Slice the celery across in thinnish pieces and thinly slice the red cabbage. Take the outer leaves and the roots off the spring onions and slice in small pieces using as much of the green stem as possible. Mix all together and dress with the yoghurt and mustard dressing made to the recipe given in Potato and Mushroom Salad.

Cucumber, Olive and Walnut Salad

Serves 6–8

Here is my adaptation of an old English recipe for an unusual and decorative cucumber salad. I find that the cream dressing instead of mayonnaise goes particularly well.

For the salad
1 medium sized cucumber
4 oz (100 g) stoned green olives – chopped
3 oz (75 g) shelled walnuts – chopped
juice of ½ lemon
a few large lettuce leaves
For the dressing
1 carton fresh soured cream
3 tablespoons (3 × 15 ml spoon) single cream
2 teaspoons (2 × 5 ml spoon) dried tarragon or chives
salt, black pepper

Peel the cucumber and chop up into cubes. Mix it in a bowl with the chopped chives, the walnuts and the lemon juice. Arrange the lettuce leaves on a serving dish and then spoon the cucumber mixture on top. Mix the dressing ingredients together until smooth and pour over the salad.

A Selection of Salads: Tomato and Sage; Celery, Red Cabbage and Spring Onion; Cucumber, Olive and Walnut

Boxing Day Sauce

Serves 6–8

A quickly made curried sauce with a beautiful sheen to it and a refreshing flavour which will revive even the driest cold turkey.

5 fl oz (125 ml) mayonnaise (a good bought kind will do)
10 fl oz (250 ml) plain yoghurt
a little orange juice (to taste)
1–3 teaspoons (1–3 × 5 ml spoon) curry powder
a little tomato purée (optional)
salt

Mix the mayonnaise and yoghurt smoothly together. Stir in the orange juice, curry powder, tomato purée and salt to taste. Either spread the sauce over a dish of carved, cold turkey or put out in a bowl for people to spoon on to their plates.

Mince Pies and Desserts

I don't think there's any comparison between homemade and shop-bought mince pies. The mincemeat can be made months ahead and looks most satisfying as it matures on the larder shelf, while the rich pastry is even more melting if you can make it in advance and keep it in your freezer. However, some people, especially children, don't really like Christmas pudding, or even mince pies, so it is good to have something sweet and refreshing but still seasonal as an alternative.

Mince Pies De Luxe

For 24 mince pies

Mince pies can be rather dry but here the mixture of the spicy mincemeat with smooth cream cheese makes them a real luxury.

8 oz (200 g) full cream cheese
2 oz (50 g) caster sugar
1 lb (400 g) orange pastry (see recipe on p.70)
1–1¼ lb (400–500 g) mincemeat
a spot of milk
caster or icing sugar for dusting

First put the cream cheese and the 2 oz caster sugar into a bowl and beat until smooth. Knead the pastry lightly and roll out rather more thickly than usual. Using a 3 in. (7 cm) fluted pastry cutter, cut out 24 rounds, re-rolling the pastry as necessary, and line greased patty tins with the rounds. Fill to about half their depth with mincemeat. Then put a teaspoonful of the beaten cream cheese mixture on top of the mincemeat and smooth over. Roll out the remaining pastry and with a smaller fluted cutter, 2¼ in. (5 cm), cut out another 24 rounds. Moisten the underside of the rounds and place them on top of the filled pies. Press the edges lightly together and make a small slit in the top of each pie. Brush with cold milk and bake in the centre of the oven, preheated to Gas Mark 7/425°F/220°C for 15–20 minutes until light golden brown. The pastry is so deliciously crumbly that it is best to let these mince pies cool down before gently easing them from the tins with a round-bladed knife.

Before serving either warm – which of course is best – or cold, sprinkle them generously with caster or icing sugar.

Mince Pies De Luxe and Traditional Mincemeat

Orange Pastry for Mince Pies

For 24 mince pies

This light, crumbly, rich pastry really compliments home-made mincemeat. To try and alleviate any last-minute panic, I always make a large batch of mince pies beforehand and put them in the freezer. I take them out and heat them up as I need them and they taste perfect.

1 lb (400 g) plain flour
8 oz (200 g) butter
4 oz (100 g) lard
grated rind of 1 large orange
orange juice

Cut the fat into the flour and rub with your fingertips until it resembles breadcrumbs. Stir in the grated rind. With a knife, stir the orange juice into the pastry until it just begins to stick together (if there isn't enough juice add a spot of cold water). Gather into a ball, wrap in foil or plastic and put into the fridge for half an hour or more before using.

Traditional Mincemeat

Makes 9–10 lb (3.5–4.0 kg)

Originally, lean beef was the important ingredient which earned this indispensable Christmas pie filling its name. I wonder why it was dropped from the recipe over the years (the first edition of Mrs Beeton is the last time we hear of it), as the beef seems to give a lovely mild taste. It makes a costlier mixture but the best I have tasted and I feel it is a tradition worth reviving. This quantity makes 9–10 lb of mincemeat, so halve the quantity if you like, though it keeps well and I find it useful for school fairs or little presents.

1 lb (400 g) seedless raisins
1½ lb (600 g) currants
¾ lb (300 g) lean rump steak – with any fat trimmed off and then minced
1½ lb (600 g) shredded beef suet
1 lb (400 g) soft dark brown sugar
4 oz (100 g) chopped mixed peel
½ whole nutmeg – freshly grated
2 lbs (800 g) cooking apples – peeled, cored and either chopped finely or minced
grated rind and juice of 1 lemon
¼ pt (125 ml) (or a little more) brandy

Thoroughly mix all the ingredients together in the order given. Stir in the lemon juice and brandy. Press closely into jars to exclude air. Leave for at least a fortnight before using.

Celebration Ice Cream

Serves 6–8

This luxurious winter ice cream made with dried fruit, nuts and port is a real treat to look forward to at Christmas. It has a beautifully rich, smooth texture and has the advantage of not having to be stirred or whisked half-way through the freezing. It is bound to make a most popular finale to one of your family feasts! If your family really don't like Christmas pudding this can be an exciting alternative.

6 oz (150 g) currants
¼ pt (125 ml) port
4 large (size 2) eggs
¼ teaspoon (½ × 2.5 ml spoon) salt
8 oz (200 g) sugar
¼ pt (125 ml) water
4 oz (100 g) shelled walnuts – roughly chopped
2 oz (50 g) chopped candied peel
2 oz (50 g) glacé cherries – roughly chopped
½ pt (250 ml) double or whipping cream
a few nuts and halved glacé cherries and angelica for decoration (optional)

Put the currants and port into a saucepan and heat to simmering. Remove from heat and leave until the port is cool. Put the eggs and salt into a mixing bowl and whisk until frothy. Put the sugar and water into a small saucepan. Bring to the boil and boil fiercely for 3 minutes. Immediately, pour this syrup in a thin stream on the frothy eggs while whisking all the time at high speed (an electric whisk is easiest for this but if you have only a hand one try to get someone else to pour the sugar syrup in, while you whisk). To help the mixture cool quickly, put the hot bowl in a sink of cold water and stir. Whip the cream until thick but not stiff. Stir the currants, port, nuts, peel and cherries into the cooled egg mixture and lastly fold in the whipped cream. Transfer to a serving bowl and freeze. When frozen decorate, if you like, with cherries, nuts and cut-out leaves of angelica.

Celebration Ice Cream

Date and Walnut Mincemeat

Makes approx. 8 lb (3 kg)

This is a good, spicy variation of the normal mincemeat mixture. It should keep well for two or three years, but if it seems to dry out add a little more rum or brandy.

8 oz (200 g) stoned dates
8 oz (200 g) raisins
8 oz (200 g) sultanas
4 oz (100 g) dried apricots or glacé cherries
8 oz (200 g) cooking apples – peeled and cored
6 oz (150 g) walnuts
4 oz (100 g) mixed peel
8 oz (200 g) shredded suet
10 oz (250 g) demerara sugar
1 level teaspoon (5 ml spoon) ground cinnamon
1 level teaspoon (5 ml spoon) ground nutmeg
1 level teaspoon (5 ml spoon) ground cloves
grated rind and juice of 2 large lemons
3–6 fl oz (75–150 ml) dark rum or brandy

Finely chop or mince the prepared fruit, peel, apples and nuts. Add the suet, sugar and spices and the grated lemon rind and juice. Stir in enough rum or brandy to give a moist mixture. Cover and leave for two days. Stir thoroughly again, put into clean jars and store in a cool place.

Dried Fruit Compote with Ginger and Rum

Serves 4–6

An excellent winter fruit salad with the most aromatic juices, which makes a refreshing dessert at Christmas time. It will keep well in the fridge.

2 × 8 oz (2 × 200 g) packets dried mixed fruit (apricots, apples, etc. – cut any extra-large fruits in half)
2 oz (50 g) crystallised ginger – cut into small pieces
2–4 oz (50–100 g) demerara or granulated sugar
juice of 2 lemons and 1 orange
2–3 tablespoons (2–3 × 15 ml spoon) dark rum

Soak the dried fruit overnight or for at least 6 hours. Drain it and put into a large saucepan with the ginger, sugar and fruit juice. Bring to the boil, then cover and simmer gently for half an hour. Then stir in the rum, transfer to a serving bowl and let cool. Serve with cream.

Snowball Pudding

Serves 6–8

I love this chilled pudding because its easy to make, looks like a snow-white Christmas pudding and tastes very good indeed. You could have it, decorated with holly, as an alternative to Christmas pudding or as a dessert at another meal. Unlike Christmas pudding, there's no question that the children might not like it – I find it universally popular.

8 oz (200 g) full cream cheese
3 oz (75 g) caster sugar
3 oz (75 g) melted unsalted butter
2 oz (50 g) chopped hazelnuts
1 oz (25 g) candied peel
2 oz (50 g) chopped glacé cherries
2 oz (50 g) chopped crystallised ginger
grated rind and juice of 2 oranges and 1 lemon
8 trifle sponges
$\frac{1}{2}$ oz (2 × 5 ml spoon) or 1 packet gelatine
$\frac{1}{4}$ pt (125 ml) double or whipping cream

Beat the cream cheese with the sugar and the melted butter until smooth and creamy. Stir in the chopped nuts, candied peel, chopped ginger and cherries and the grated rind of the oranges and lemon. Slice the sponges crossways into 3 thin slices each. Put 3 or 4 slices on the bottom of a 2-pt pudding basin. Then spoon a layer of the cream cheese mixture, then another layer of sponges, and so on, ending with a layer of sponges. Dilute the juice of the oranges and lemon to $\frac{3}{4}$ pt (375 ml), with hot water. Dissolve the gelatine in a cup with 2 tablespoons of very hot water and stir it into the juices. Strain the juice over the mixture in the pudding basin, making sure the juice gets to the bottom of the basin by pulling the mixture back with a spoon.

Put in the fridge to set. When well chilled, dip the basin briefly in hot water and turn out on to a serving plate. Whisk the cream until thick and ice the pudding with it. Decorate the top with a sprig of holly. Chill again in the fridge before serving.

Snowball Pudding

Seasonal Cakes

However much food you have over Christmas the decorated cake, like the Christmas tree, is something you can't really do without. However, as long as its decorated appearance evokes Christmas cheer, it doesn't have to be a solid traditional cake covered with thick marzipan and rock-hard icing. Here are some mouthwatering alternatives.

Yule Log

Serves 6–8

You may prefer, like the French, to have a rich chocolate log at Christmas instead of Christmas cake (or have it as well). This one, made with ground hazelnuts instead of flour, is light and luscious.

5 large (size 4) eggs – separated
5 oz (125 g) caster sugar
3 oz (75 g) ground hazelnuts (whizz up the whole nuts for a moment in either a liquidiser or coffee grinder) *or* ground almonds
1½ level teaspoons (3 × 2.5 ml spoon) baking powder
2 rounded tablespoons (3 × 15 ml spoon) cocoa powder, finely sifted
2–3 tablespoons (2–3 × 15 ml spoon) warm water
¼ teaspoon (½ × 2.5 ml spoon) cream of tartar
icing sugar
apricot jam
½ pt (250 ml) double cream

Heat the oven to Gas Mark 4/350°F/180°C. Lightly oil a large swiss roll tin measuring approximately 14 in. × 10 in. (35 cm × 25 cm). Line the bottom with a piece of greaseproof paper, also lightly oiled. Whisk the yolks of the eggs with the sugar until pale and fairly thick, but not stiff. Stir in the hazelnuts, baking powder and the cocoa powder and add the water to soften the mixture. Add the cream of tartar to the egg whites and whisk until stiff. Using a metal spoon, fold them gently but thoroughly into the yolk mixture.

Pour into the prepared tin and bake in the centre of the oven for about 20–25 minutes until springy to touch in the centre. Remove the tin from the oven, and leave to cool. The cake will now shrink a little, but that's normal. When cool, cover with greaseproof paper and a cloth and leave in the fridge for 2–3 hours, or overnight if possible. Then loosen the edges carefully with a knife.

Sprinkle a piece of greaseproof paper generously with sieved icing sugar. Turn the cake out on to the icing sugar and remove the oiled paper. Spread with apricot jam. Whip the cream until thick and spread on top of the jam. Roll up with the help of the greaseproof paper, carefully and rather loosely. It will probably crack a bit but the cracks make it look like a real snow-covered log. Transfer to a serving dish. Sprinkle more icing sugar all over through a sieve and decorate with red-berried holly.

Seasonal Cakes: Yule Log, Black Bun and Glossy Fruit and Walnut Christmas Cake

Glossy Fruit and Walnut Christmas Cake

Serves 6–8

If, like my family, you can easily do without marzipan and the hard icing covering of the Christmas cake, and find the cake itself rather too similar to the Christmas pudding, here is an alternative which is much less trouble and can look equally festive. It is a dark, moist cake, packed with fruit and nuts. Make it several weeks in advance if possible.

For the cake
8 oz (200 g) raisins
4 oz (100 g) currants
4 oz (100 g) sultanas
6 oz (150 g) dried apricots – chopped into small pieces
2 oz (50 g) mixed peel
3–4 tablespoons (3–4 × 15 ml spoon) rum or brandy
8 oz (200 g) self-raising flour
good pinch of salt
½ whole nutmeg – grated
6 oz (150 g) soft dark brown sugar
6 oz (150 g) butter
8 oz (200 g) chopped walnuts
2 large (size 4) beaten eggs
1 tablespoon (15 ml spoon) black treacle dissolved in a tablespoon of warm milk
For the glaze and decoration
angelica
glacé cherries
¾ lb (300 g) redcurrant jelly
preserving sugar or coffee sugar crystals
silver balls (optional)

The night before you make the cake put the fruit with the rum or brandy in a bowl, stir well together, put a cloth on top and leave overnight. The next day, heat the oven to Gas Mark 4/350°F/180°C. Grease and line a 8–9 in. (20–22 cm) round cake tin with greased greaseproof paper.

Put the flour, salt, nutmeg and sugar into a mixing bowl. Cut the butter into small lumps and rub it well into the flour and sugar with your fingers. Stir in the fruit, alcohol, and the chopped walnuts. Thoroughly stir in the beaten eggs and then the treacle dissolved in milk.

Put the mixture into the cake tin and bake in the centre of the oven. After half an hour turn the oven down to Gas Mark 2/300°F/150°C for about another 1¼–1¾ hours until a sharp knife stuck into the centre comes out clean. If the cake looks as if it is getting too brown place a sheet of foil or brown paper on the top. Remove from the oven and leave in the tin for about 5 minutes, then loosen the edges carefully with a knife and turn out the right way up on a cooling tray. When cool, wrap in two layers of greaseproof paper and then in a double layer of foil and store in a cool place.

A day or two before Christmas wash the excess sugar from the angelica under water and pat dry with a cloth. Then cut out holly leaves if you can or just ordinary diamond leaf shapes. Cut a few glacé cherries in half. Then gently melt the redcurrant jelly in a pan and brush it all over the cake. Immediately arrange the angelica leaves and halved cherries in a pattern on top and sprinkle the sugar crystals all around. The crystals look like ice or frost and I also dot silver balls around the top and sides of the cake, which gives an added sparkle.

Dark Chocolate Cake

Serves 6–8

It has now become a tradition in our family to have this moist chocolate cake instead of the usual rich fruit cake at Christmas time. After the fruit-filled pudding and mince pies we all much prefer it and with its snowy-white frosting the appearance when decorated is perfectly seasonal.

For the cranberry and orange filling
4 fl oz (100 ml) fresh orange juice (about 2 oranges)
4 oz (100 g) sugar
8 oz (200 g) fresh cranberries
For the cake
4 oz (100 g) plain chocolate
3 tablespoons (3 × 15 ml spoon) water
6 oz (150 g) butter or margarine
10 oz (250 g) soft dark brown sugar
1 teaspoon (5 ml spoon) vanilla essence
3 large (size 4) eggs – lightly whisked
6 fl oz (150 ml) milk soured by adding the juice of ½ lemon
10 oz (250 g) plain flour
½ teaspoon (2.5 ml spoon) baking powder
1½ level teaspoons (3 × 2.5 ml spoon) bicarbonate of soda
For the frosting
2 large (size 4) egg whites
12 oz (300 g) caster sugar
good pinch of salt
juice of 1 lemon
1 tablespoon (15 ml spoon) water
½ teaspoon (2.5 ml spoon) cream of tartar
Christmas decorations

Make the filling first. Put the orange juice in a saucepan and stir in the sugar. Add the cranberries. Cover, bring to the boil and simmer for 5 minutes. Cool and chill well in the fridge before using.

Now line two greased $8\frac{1}{2}$–$9\frac{1}{2}$ in. (22–24 cm) sandwich tins with greased greaseproof paper. Break the chocolate into

Dark Chocolate Cake for Christmas

small pieces, then put with the 3 spoons of hot water in a bowl over a pan of very hot water, stirring occasionally until smooth. Remove from the heat and cool slightly. Turn the oven to Gas Mark 4/350°F/180°C. Cream the fat with the sugar and vanilla essence until light and fluffy. Thoroughly beat in the eggs and melted chocolate. Add the soured milk alternately with the sifted flour, baking powder and bicarbonate of soda. Divide the mixture between the two tins and smooth with a knife. Bake towards the centre of the oven for 30–40 minutes until well risen and springy to touch in the centre. Leave in the tins for 10 minutes, then turn the cakes carefully out on to a wire tray to cool, and remove greaseproof paper. When cold, sandwich together with the cranberry and orange filling.

To make the frosting, put all the ingredients together in a large deep bowl and whisk together. Put the bowl over a pan of very hot water and continue to whisk for about 10 minutes until the mixture is thick enough to stand in peaks and the sugar has dissolved. Spread at once thickly all over the cake with a wide knife, making rough flicks, decorate, leave in a cool place but not the fridge. You can, of course, make the cake in advance and freeze it. The icing is best done a day before you cut the cake.

Black Bun

Serves 8–10

In Scotland, as the clock strikes midnight on New Year's Eve, you cut your black bun and offer it around with a glass of whisky. It is a dark, succulent and concentrated mass of fruit, nuts and spices mixed with a lot of whisky, bound with very little flour and egg and sealed in a crisp pastry case. Needless to say, it is delicious and should be made weeks or months ahead to allow it to mature.

For the pastry
8 oz (200 g) plain flour
pinch of salt
4 oz (100 g) butter
egg yolk to glaze
For the filling
1 lb (400 g) currants
1 lb (400 g) raisins
2 oz (50 g) candied peel
4 oz (100 g) chopped or flaked blanched almonds
4 oz (100 g) plain flour
4 oz (100 g) soft brown sugar
1 teaspoon (5 ml spoon) each of ground cinnamon, ginger, allspice or cloves and nutmeg
1 level teaspoon (5 ml spoon) cream of tartar
1 level teaspoon (5 ml spoon) bicarbonate of soda
1 lightly whisked egg
8 tablespoons (8 × 15 ml spoon) whisky
3 level tablespoons (3 × 15 ml spoon) black treacle

Grease an 8 in. (20 cm) round cake tin. Make the pastry in the usual way. Leave to rest while you mix up the filling. Mix all the dry ingredients for the filling together in a large bowl. Stir in the egg and whisky. Melt the treacle in a pan to make it runny and stir it in.

Roll out two-thirds of the pastry into a circle about 14 in. (35 cm) in diameter. Line the cake tin with it, making sure the pastry comes up above the top of the sides of the tin. Spoon the filling in and level it. Fold the top of the pastry over. Roll out the remaining pastry to an 8 in. (20 cm) circle – you can put the tin on the pastry and cut it round to make an even circle. Moisten the edges of the pastry, put on the circle lid and press the edges firmly together. I use leftover bits of pastry to decorate and to write "Happy New Year" in cut-out letters, which makes the glazed black bun look most impressive. Lastly, with a skewer, make 4 or 5 holes right down to the bottom of the cake, then prick all over the top with a fork and brush with egg yolk.

Bake in the centre of the oven at Gas Mark 4/350°F/180°C for 2½–3 hours. When the pastry turns a rich golden brown lay a piece of foil on top so it doesn't get any darker. Turn carefully out of the tin and cool. Store in an airtight tin or wrapped in foil in a cool place.

Seasonal Drinks

"Whene'er a bowl of punch we make,
Four striking opposites we take:
The strong, the weak, the sour, the sweet,
Together mixed most kindly meet:
And when they happily unite
The bowl is pregnant with delight."

In spite of this rhyme, which I found in an old cookery book, the word punch comes from the Indian word *panch* meaning five – *i.e.*, five ingredients. However, there are all sorts of punches, with varying numbers of ingredients, and you may well have your own concoction. Their warm, spicy, potent taste is especially appropriate at Christmas time. Even those who usually dislike sweet things can enjoy a traditional, aromatic brew round the Christmas tree.

Glühwein

For about 6 people

This Austrian way of mulling wine is specially good for parties, as it has a nice fresh taste and transforms cheap wine.

1 large (1 litre) bottle cheap red wine
3–4 oz (75–100 g) sugar, to taste
1 teaspoon (5 ml spoon) whole cloves
1 teaspoon (5 ml spoon) ground cinnamon
juice of 1 orange and 1 lemon

Pour the wine into a saucepan. Add the other ingredients. Heat until nearly boiling, then strain into a warmed bowl and serve.

Old-fashioned Mulled Wine

For about 6 people

A traditional recipe for a delicious, warming brew.

1 large (1 litre) bottle Spanish red wine
10 fl oz (250 ml) ginger ale or cold strained tea
1 orange, stuck with 10 cloves
3 cinnamon sticks or 1 teaspoon (5 ml spoon) cinnamon powder
2 teaspoons (2 × 5 ml spoon) mixed spice
4 oz (100 g) brown sugar
large wineglass brandy *or* whisky *or* dark rum

Put all ingredients in a pan and heat thoroughly, without boiling, for about half an hour. Before serving add the brandy, whisky or rum.

Cider Punch

For about 10 people

Here is a cheering punch which isn't too expensive.

2 pts (1 litre) sweet cider
1 teaspoon (5 ml spoon) each ground cinnamon and nutmeg
juice of 1 lemon

Put the ingredients in a pan, bring to the boil and simmer for about 5 minutes. Serve immediately.

Non-alcoholic Punch for Children's Parties

For about 10 people

This refreshing, non-alcoholic punch is ideal for children's parties during the festive season – or at any time.

2 pts (1 litre) sugar syrup (1¼ pt (625 ml) water and 12 oz (300 g) sugar)
2 pts (1 litre) water
1 pt (½ litre) orange juice
½ pt (¼ litre) grapefruit juice
1 teaspoon (5 g) each of ground ginger and cinnamon
8 cloves
mint and fruit to decorate, according to season

Boil together for 5 minutes the sugar syrup, water and spices to extract the flavour. Add the orange and grapefruit juice and stir well. Serve either hot or chilled, decorated with mint and fruit, whatever is in season.

Christmas Cheer – a Wassail Cup

For about 10 people

If you have no personal concoction to warm the spirit at Christmas time and want to stick to old traditions, drink the health of your family and friends round the Wassail bowl on Christmas Eve or Twelfth Night. But remember to sing, too!

4 oz (100 g) sugar
3 cinnamon sticks or 2 teaspoons (2 × 5 ml spoon) ground cinnamon
½ pt (250 ml) pineapple juice
½ pt (250 ml) orange juice
juice of 2–3 lemons
5 fl oz (125 ml) dry sherry
2½–3 pts (1.25–1.5 litres) ale
slices of lemon

Boil up the sugar, cinnamon and fruit juice together for 5 minutes. Pour the sherry and ale into a large pan and strain the fruit juice mixture into it. Heat but don't boil. Garnish with slices of lemon and serve.

Wassail Cup

Christmas Wines – What to Drink with What

The rule about drink, as about food, is do what you like and try out new combinations. All that matters is that you please yourself and your family. Christmas is a time when most of us buy more drink than usual, and it is a special treat to serve a number of different wines with a meal. Christmas is one time you can do it without having expensive bottles left over, because you can as easily serve six people with a different bottle for each course, as three bottles of the same wine, which may go well with the turkey, but will taste a bit odd with the first courses, or the Christmas pudding. Here are a few ideas. I have just mentioned the type of wine I think goes well with each dish. Obviously, how good a wine you buy of each kind is a matter of choice.

With snacks, Aubergine Purée, etc, for friends who drop in
Apart from spirits and soft drinks (it is surprising how many people ask for cola or ginger beer) it is worth having Macon Blanc – dry and sharp. Serve well chilled. My favourite is the fragrant Chambery Vermouth, with ice and a slice of lemon. And, of course, sherry – Manzanilla, with its slightly salty taste, specially good with fish dishes or the smoky Aubergine Purée, or a Fino.

With the turkey
Nothing can beat a good claret. It has the right weight for turkey – not so light that it gets lost, not so heavy that the turkey is outdone. For this reason I prefer it to Burgundy or Beaujolais.

Some people prefer dry white wine or a Riesling or hock with turkey on the old-fashioned grounds that white wine and white meat go together. I think this is a mistake. Don't, whatever you do, forget to put the red wine in a warm room the night before and open it at least a couple of hours before drinking. The cheaper the red wine the *more* it benefits from being opened early to let the air get at it. Decanting it helps, too.

With the Christmas pudding or the Christmas cake

Try not to go on drinking the red wine with the Christmas pudding. It is too sharp and can be too light. Christmas pudding is rich and needs a rich sweet wine to set it off. Buy a Sauternes or French sweet white wine, chill it well in the fridge for two or three hours and you will be astonished how delicious it tastes – even quite a cheap bottle. You could also try a rich Muscatel with the pudding, or even a cream sherry, but save port for the nuts and fruit at the end of the meal.

Champagne or sparkling wine

It is really worth buying a bottle or two of Champagne or one of the many sparkling wines now on the market. Just the sight of the bubbles and the pale golden colour cheers up jaded spirits. You can drink it at any time – before lunch, with the Christmas pudding, at the end of the meal, when everyone feels rather full, or after the children have been put to bed and you are in need of a pick-me-up. It does not matter when you drink it, but to have it is to add a final touch to the celebrations, and when you work out the cost of a sparkling white wine, you will find it is no more expensive than pouring gin and tonic.

With cold food and leftovers

I have tried to suggest ways of making cold meat and salad different and enticing on Boxing Day and through the holiday. But if you are going to take trouble with that, take trouble with the wine too. To drink the same wine you drank on Christmas Day is like serving leftovers.

Try a cold rosé – for instance, you may like the slightly sweet Rosé d'Anjou. Or chill a bottle of red wine – a Beaujolais does well. It tastes quite different from when it is warm – refreshing and brisk-tasting. A Côte du Rhône, with its slightly flinty taste, also goes well with cold meat. If you want a white wine a fresh Vouvray or a light dry white Spanish wine would do well. If your guests do not want to drink anything too heavy add soda water to the Spanish white wine, to make it light and sparkling.

Do try to remember to make sure the white wines are really cool. They lose a lot if they are served too warm. Don't be afraid to put a lump of ice in them if the worst comes to the worst – though it is better to find a container that can act as an ice bucket.

If you have anything left in your budget I would lay in a stock of beer and lager, and buy a small bottle of liqueur, perhaps cherry brandy, as a luxury to drink with your coffee. And a bottle of Perrier water, or another sparkling water, which served with a slice of lemon and ice looks, and is, healthy and restoring, particularly when you've eaten too much.